cah

Angelic Magic with the Kabbalistic Angel cahetEL

FRATER EISENHEIM

For ELOHIM, the creator of the heavens, the earth and all creatures, all the glory for him.

For my Angel of the day MAHASIAH, for my Angel of the hour IMAMIAH, for my Angel of the Zodiac BARCHIEL and for my Archangel MICHAEL, gratitude to all of you!

To the Kabbalistic Angel of the Sun Ariel (46º), for having manifested himself to me, after SEVERAL unsuccessful attempts, gratitude!

To Lalá (In Memory)

Dedication

Who are you? Apparently it is a simple question, you can answer that you are a doctor, an engineer or a lawyer, but in fact, who are you? What did you come to do in the material world? Passing a prescription, building bridges or defending innocent people, who are you? Questions like these hang in the heads of human beings every day and finding the answer is not an easy task, perhaps you will only know the answer when you disincarnate and until then you may suffer the pain of the absence of the answer. My dear reader, living hurts, certainly some people will say that it doesn't hurt if you are a billionaire, billionaires also feel pain, the pain of the mother's absence who is gone too soon, the pain of not being able to participate in the growth of a child , living really hurts and I will tell the noble readers a little story.

On October 29, 1978, a boy is born in a city in the Northeast, what does that have too much? Nothing, hundreds, thousands, millions of boys were born on that day, but maybe all the boys who were born on that day were not born 2 more times later. The boy who was born 3 times, until the age of 14, had an abundant life, but due to the lack of wisdom of the family patriarch, the abundance was gone and the difficult times came. The boy then started to live only with his mother, without the presence of a father of any kind and after a certain time, they moved to another city in the Northeast and the boy's mother started to work as a cleaner to support 3 children. . Not enduring such difficulty, the matriarch of the family returns to the city of origin with everyone, to be close to the family that has always been present.

The boy, whom I will call Michael, grew up and managed to have access to a decent education, just like his brothers and there was a question that always remained deep in Michael's heart: Who am I? No answers.

The years passed, one night Michael left the house to go for a drive with his friends. On the way back, the friend in the back seat asked Michael to get down in the passenger seat, because he was too far ahead and The driver next to him could not see the right rearview mirror and Michael did so, lowered the seat so that the driver could see the rearview mirror. On the way home, the driver of the car completely lost control of the steering, Michael when seeing that he would have an accident at that moment only did one thing: Close your eyes. When opening, there was a gigantic tree in the middle of the car, because the collision had occurred on the side that Michael was on, the collision was so strong, that the car was completely destroyed, but Michael, the friend in the back seat and the driver left unscathed from the accident, without any scratches and what most caught Michael's attention: If it weren't for the friend from the back seat, the tree would have hit Michael on the head, but it didn't hit because he tilted the seat. The next day, life goes on and in moments of reflection Michael asked himself: Why didn't I die? Who am I? No answers.

Time goes by, Michael is already a man and on another occasion he goes out with friends for an event. At the end of the event, a friend offers a ride to Michael and because of the schedule asks him to go to sleep at his house, the next day Michael would go home and Michael accepts the invitation. Leaving the event site, a football arena where a part was still under construction, Michael stumbles and I crashed hitting my head on a stone, very close to the back of the neck, not even passing out, but losing a lot of blood and at the moment of the incident begins raining very hard, second only to the flood of Noah, Michael is alone lying on the floor bleeding and his friend desperate not knowing what to do and it took about 10 minutes, behold, a girl appears and the girl presses on Michael's head so that the blood stops flowing and both friends take Michael to a hospital close to home, when he arrives at the hospital, the doctor congratulated Michael for being born a second time, because if it was a little further down the stroke, he would hit the back of the head and it would certainly lead the boy to death and he corrected the doctor, saying that it was his third and not his second birth, which shocked everyone who was in the clinic. The next day, life goes on and in moments of reflection Michael asked himself: Why didn't I die? Who am I? My life did not leave the corner, everything I do does not work, all friends have evolved, they are very well and I am stagnant and Elohim wants me alive, why? No answers.

Michael continues his journey without answers and starts living with his grandmother, the years go by, Michael loves his grandmother's company, only the two of them live and a domestic help, his grandmother occasionally had nightmares during the night and Michael woke up and was going to wake up his grandmother who screamed in fear of the nightmare and this was repeated for several years and that intrigued Michael. One day, his grandmother complained of abdominal pain, but they didn't take it too seriously and the pain continued, one day the grandmother had to have surgery and when starting the medical procedure, they discovered a terminal cancer in the intestine, ended the surgery , they called Michael's family and gave the fateful news, at the most 6 months of life and as his grandmother was hypertensive and was already over 80 years old, she could not know about the disease, because if she knew not even 6 months she would live and if she lived , would not resist treatment, because of age. Michael's grandmother returns home and continues to live with him, with the help of domestic services, family and abdominal pains, taking endorphins every day to pass the pains and without knowing what he had and Michael wondered: I'm going to get beat up of life forever? No answers.

One night, the grandmother does not feel well and is taken to the hospital by the family, the disease had evolved and Michael's visits to the grandmother become painful, shortly after she enters the ICU and they tell Michael the night at the grandmother's house, he wasn't in the habit of talking to Yod, but that night he asked for her pain to end and went to sleep afterwards, the next day he was woken by his mother to go to the hospital to say goodbye to her grandmother, she was dying and she died, at least it was attended to.

On a Christmas night, the whole family would gather at the grandmother's house and there would be a distribution of gifts, each person present donated a value, with the amount that was collected, several Christmas kits were assembled and the draw would be as follows, the participant takes a piece of paper containing a word from a sock and that word will give the participant the corresponding kit.

Michael in financial difficulty, was left out, because he cannot contribute with the amount, but when each one removed the paper from the sock, a cousin called him in a corner of the wall and said that he would participate, Michael did not want to accept, because he hadn't contributed, but his cousin insisted he had to participate.
As they took the paper out of the sock, I started saying what word was written and they took the corresponding kit, finally Michael's time to take the paper off him and show the word to his family, the word he took out of the bag this was the next one.

(Light in Portuguese)

Michael goes to the bathroom and cries.

The story of the boy Michael is a true story, he continues to search for answers and his life remains stagnant, but do you know why he did not go into depression and did not shoot himself in the head? Because he has something that a lot of people are either losing or have already lost: FAITH! Michael continues the journey of life, living and knowing that one day the answers will come, but living hurts like it hurts, literally.

I dedicate this book to you, who have not lost FAITH, who know that their time will come, because they know that Elohim does not abandon his children, the children of Israel were enslaved for 400 years in Egypt, but they did not lose FAITH in God. of Abraham and the God of Abraham took Moses and resolved slavery in Egypt! To have FAITH is not to be assiduous in religious worship, I know a religious who jumped off a bridge because he suffered from depression, to have FAITH and not to take away the most precious thing that Adonai gave us: Life. Having FAITH is that you do not shoot yourself in the head when NOTHING works, but you keep trying, that is having FAITH, I wish from the bottom of my heart that you find out who you are.

"Hope for the Lord, be strong and He will give your heart courage, and hope for the Lord."

Psalms 27:14

"But I trusted in You, O Lord; I said, "You are my God."

Psalms 31:15

"Trust in the Lord and do good; dwell in the land and be nourished by faith. So shall you delight in the Lord, and He will give you what your heart desires."

Psalms 37:3-4

"A prayer of Moses, the man of God. O Lord, You have been our dwelling place throughout all generations. Before the mountains were born, and You brought forth the earth and the inhabited world, and from everlasting to everlasting, You are God. You bring man to the crushing point, and You say, "Return, O sons of men." For a thousand years are in Your eyes like yesterday, which passed, and a watch in the night. You carry them away as a flood; they are like a sleep; in the morning, like grass it passes away. In the morning, it blossoms and passes away; in the evening, it is cut off and withers."

Index

Introduction

"I want to teach you to address the Creator, instead of addressing me, because He is the only force, the only source of everything that exists, the only one who can really help you and who expects your pleas for help. Only the Creator can offer you support in the search for the formula to free yourself from the bondage of this world, help to rise above it, help in discovering your being and in determining the purpose of your life. The Creator is the one who sends you all these aspirations, in order to compel you to address Him. "

Rabbi Baruch Shalom Halevi Ashlag

Chapter 1

Place of Practice and Instruments

It is convenient to set aside an environment exclusively for contact with the ultra, far from external influences, curious looks, let alone those who condemn, the ignorant of a skeptical nature, those who cannot understand because their time has not yet come or because they are not in their destination the Master.

It is essential to understand that the place for the practice is of concentration, meditation, invocation, evocation, etc., becomes a living organism. On one side, consciousness changes, rises, and on the other, the skies go down to the operator. Nothing that happens there is by chance. Certainly, there will be manifestations that at first can be frightening, but with time everything becomes so natural that something may go unnoticed - it is necessary to be very careful in this sense: getting used to the supernatural.

We know that not everyone has such a room, so I will describe how is our place of evocative practices, our altars and our instruments, is the reader obliged to have all this? For invocations no, for evocations yes, first you must understand the 4 quadrants, they are:

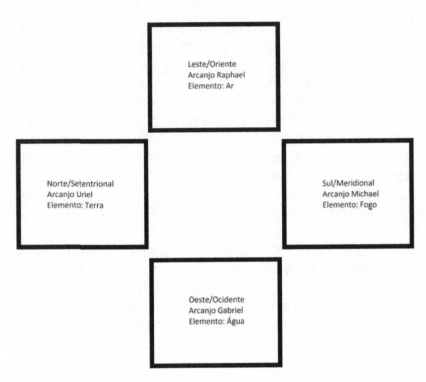

When we speak facing the East, you already know where to put yourself and you should always follow the clockwise direction, that is, East (Start) -> South-> West-> North-> East (End), if you have difficulty finding the 4 cardinal points, I suggest you install on your smartphone a digital compass (App), there are several in the app stores.

Raphael's (רָפָאֵל) altar on East

A small altar should be created for the Archangel Raphael with stones, incense, candles and plants, give preference to a Jewish candlestick with seven arms, as described by the ETERNAL to Moses:

"And you shall make a menorah of pure gold. The menorah shall be made of hammered work; its base and its stem, its goblets, its knobs, and its flowers shall [all] be [one piece] with it."

Exodus 25:31

"And you shall make its lamps seven, and he shall kindle its lamps [so that they] shed light toward its face."

Exodus 25:37

A small table containing:

1. An Image of Raphael made of plaster or other material, if you can't get an image of him from the internet, print it out and put it in a frame;
2. Raphael's stamp, made by you and your hand on a piece of pine wood, if you don't

have the wood, draw it on a never-used piece of A4 paper, as follows:

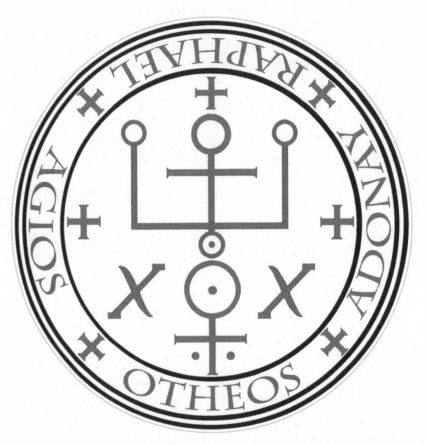

3. An orange towel;
4. A Jewish Menorah;

5. 7 orange candles;
6. At least 1 Almécega Incense, White Sandalwood, Galbanum;
7. At least 1 Marjoram Plant, Fennel, Mandrake, Caraway, Dill, Pomegranate, Palm, White Mistletoe, Dandelion, Mint, Lavender, Golden Rod;
8. At least 1 Opal Stone, Fire Opal, Agate, Serpentine, Topaz.

Michael's (מִיכָאֵל) Altar on South

Likewise, create a small altar for the Archangel Michael containing:

1. An Image of Michael made of plaster or other material, if you can't get an image of him from the internet, print it out and put it in a frame;
2. Michael's stamp, made by you and your hand on a piece of pine wood, if you don't have the wood, draw it on a never-used piece of A4 paper, as follows:

3. A yellow towel;
4. A Jewish Menorah;
5. 7 yellow candles;
6. At least 1 Frankincense, Cinnamon Incense;

7. At least 1 Plant of Ash, Mustard, Cactus, Pepper, Garlic, Onion, Thistle, Sunflower, Acacia, Laurel, Wonder, Saffron, Rowan, Peony;
8. At least 1 Ruby Stone, Fire Opal, Topaz, Chrysolite, Heliotrope, Zircon;
9. Some Gold object.

Gabriel's (גבריאל) Altar on West

Likewise, create a small altar for the archangel Gabriel containing:

1. An Image of Gabriel made of plaster or other material, if you can't get an image of him from the internet, print it out and put it in a frame;
2. Gabriel's stamp, made by you and your hand on a piece of pine wood, if you don't have the wood, draw it on a never-used piece of A4 paper, as follows:

3. A White or Silver towel;
4. A Jewish Menorah;
5. 7 white or silver candles;
6. At least 1 Incense from Onicha, Myrrh, Camphor, Aloe;

7. At least 1 Lotus Plant, Melon, Orchid, Gardenia, Mushroom, Poppy;
8. At least 1 Aquamarine Stone, Coral, Moon Stone, Pearl, Quartz, Fluorite;
9. Some silver object.

Uriel's (אוריאל) Altar on North

Likewise, create a small altar for the archangel Gabriel containing:

1. An Image of Uriel made of plaster or other material, if you can't get an image of him from the internet, print it out and put it in a frame;
2. Uriel's stamp, made by you and your hand on a piece of pine wood, if you don't have the wood, draw it on a never-used piece of A4 paper, as follows:

3. A Green Towel;
4. Uma menorá judaica;
5. 7 green candles;
6. At least 1 Starach Incense
7. At least 1 Oak Plant, Cypress, Grain, Potato, Turnip, Cotton, Patchouli;

8. At least 1 Moss Agate Stone, Salt Stone, Onyx, Galena

The Main Altar on East

Put on East:

1. 3 candles (fire element), one above and two below, forming a triangle;
2. In the middle of the triangle, the manifestation board (explained later);
3. In the center of the demonstration board, his crystal ball (crystal and not glass);
4. 2 boxes of incense (air element) with two different perfumes, usually each box contains 7 sticks, burn the 7 sticks to the left of the triangle and the other 7 sticks to the right of the triangle;
5. 1 crystal bowl with mineral water (water element);
6. 1 container with earth (earth element).
7. The angel's seal;

The Board of Manifestations

The board was made following the work of the renowned occult Master Trithemius of Spanheim, where it describes how to attract spirits into crystals where it is found on a magic board, I modified this board for the purpose of the 72 kabbalistic spirits.

The Crystal Ball

You should get a good crystal, clear and transparent, at least five centimeters in diameter.

It must be spherical in shape, with a perfectly regular globe. When you are in possession of this crystal, pure and clear, without the slightest stain or opacity, you will need to activate the crystal, when the moon is growing, place the crystal in a place where it receives the energies of the 7 planets and leave it there for 7 days , starting on a Sunday and ending on a Sunday, after 7 days remove the crystal from the place and say out loud the following prayer:

"Oh Lord, my God, who is the author of all good things, fortify me, I invoke you, I who am a humble servant, so that I can pass without harm, without fear, through this work and this contact, enlighten , oh Lord, I implore you, the dark-filled intellect of your creature, so that the eyes of your spirit can open, see and know your angelic spirit that will descend on this crystal "

Put your right hand on the crystal and keep saying:

"And you, oh inanimate creature of God, be sanctified, consecrated, and blessed by this office, and let no evil specter appear in you; and if anyone gets to penetrate this creature he may be forced to speak intelligibly and sincerely, without double meaning or ambiguity, in the name of Our Lord Jesus Christ. Amen".

"Your servant who is before you oh Lord, does not desire corrupt treasures, nor the evil of his neighbors, nor the harm of any living being. Grant

it, for the power to discern those spirits or terrestrial intelligences that may appear in this crystal and those beneficial gifts that your generosity wishes to bestow (such as the power to cure illnesses, or to infuse wisdom, or to bring all evil to light that may afflict any person or family, or any other precious gift) grant the Lord, who knows how to implore thanks to your wisdom and mercy, in order to receive the honor of your holy name. Grant him all this for the love of your Son Jesus Christ. Amen".

Your crystal is almost ready to receive the geniuses, next step is to consecrate the same, do as described in the chapter on exorcism and consecration.

The Manifestation

Wait for the angel to manifest itself in the crystal ball, if it does not manifest itself in the crystal ball, be aware of your surroundings, it may manifest itself in the smoke of the incense, or in the flame of the candle, be aware, the manifestation sometimes happens and we don't notice, but I warn the reader, the spirit that was evoked is not always manifested, but other spirits, that's why we should ask whoever is manifested, when he reaches the crystal ball, talk to him, his answers will come your mind, you speak normal, as if you were talking to a human and he will answer you mentally.

Looking at the ball say:

"In the name of the Sacred and incorruptible Spirit of the father, of his Son begotten in the womb of Mary and of the Holy Spirit, what is your true name, spirit?"

If the spirit is silent ask again until he answers, if he does not answer at all, do Appendix VI, VII and I in sequence, do not change the sequence, if the spirit responds with his correct name, then continue.

"Do you want to swear by the blood of Jesus Christ of Nazareth killed on the cross that you truly are (NAME OF THE ANGEL EVOKED)?"

If you are silent and do not answer at all, do Appendix VI, VII and I in sequence, do not change the sequence, if the spirit answers YES, then continue.

"What are your virtues?"

Talk to him (do not abuse the time, maximum 20 minutes, be direct in the questions and the main thing, I always respect him, he's holy you don't) and also write down all the things he decides to teach you, each answer you give to your questions and when finished, recite to him the specific prayer of the angel that is in each described ritual.

Dee and Kelley, 16x20, oil on canvas, by S. Haines 2010

Consulting the Tarot

It's good to always check the tarot to see if the material is really consecrated or if something went wrong, if you don't want to use it, there's no problem, but I recommend you use it, to avoid walking in the dark thinking that something is consecrated and in truth is not. I use the Egyptian deck, you can use another oracle as long as it has 22 major arcana and 56 minor arcana.

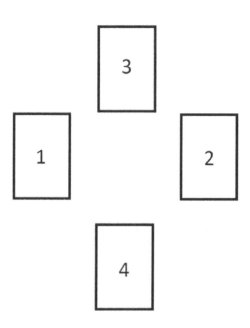

You should choose this method of disposition whenever you want the Tarot to accompany you through the process of reaching a goal, or if you are looking for a guide to take you through even the most complicated paths. It doesn't tell you where the path will lead in the end, but what to do next. As the cards always refer, according to our experience, to a time span of almost no more than 14 days, this is the most suitable game for subjects on which you want to consult the cards several times, in order to receive new ones again and again. impulses. Also, in this case, the tarot itself tells you when to look at the cards again.

The meaning of each position:

1 = The starting situation. Where the querent is at the moment;
2 = This is not important right now. This is not to be feared or expected;
3 = Only this matters now;
4 = The next step leads to this. Once this happens, it's time to look at the cards again.

Making the consultation:

1. Light a white candle and myrrh incense;
2. Shuffle the entire deck with the figures facing down, without seeing the figures;
3. Spread the entire deck on the table;
4. Remove one card, face down and place it in position 1, remove another card, face down and place it in position 2, remove another card face down and place it in position 3 and to finish remove one more card with the figure face down and place it in position 4;

5. Time to turn the cards in positions 1,2,3 and 4 in the sequence, do not change the sequence, leaving the figure face up.
6. Time to interpret the cards in each position.

Cards 1 and 4 show the starting point and where the next step leads. Card 4 should not be given an exaggerated meaning here. It basically indicates when to lay the cards down again, that is, when the step described here has been taken. This is the moment when the experience described by card 4 takes place, even if it lasts only a few minutes. The most important card is in position 3. It indicates what to look out for during this entire period of time, what will really take you forward. Card 2 is somewhat of a warning, as all the energy that flows in that direction will be wasted. This is because the situation outlined in this letter will most certainly not happen during this process.

"I believe in God the Father, creator of heaven and earth, of all that can and cannot be seen."

O Ritual

"Remember, he knows you, he knows all your sins and secrets. You are not alone, he will always be with you!"

O Ritual

"Be careful, not believing in the Devil won't protect you from him. The terror is real, it's real. But you'll only defeat it when you believe!"

O Ritual

"There are times when I experience total loss of faith. Days, months when I don't know what to believe. God or Devil, Santa Claus or Tink, but I'm just a man and a weak man, I have no power, but at the same time time something keeps digging and scraping inside me. It seems to be the nail of God. And finally I can't take the pain any longer and I'm thrown out of the darkness and back into the light. Ex umbris ad lucem."

O Ritual

Chapter 2

Exorcism and Consecration

In order to be successful in an evocation ritual, one must exorcise ALL the material and consecrate after that, the best day to do it is on a Wednesday of a crescent or full moon at the hour of mercury, or on the day and hour of the ruling planet, for example, consecrate yellow candle (color of the sun), consecrate in the day and time of the sun when the moon is growing or full, consecrate white candle (color of the moon), consecrate in the day and time of the moon when the moon is growing or full, consecrate the crystal ball, make the consecration on the day and time of mercury when the moon is growing or full, that is, when it is from a planet to do it on the day and time of that planet and when there is no planet to do in the day and time of mercury, always in the period of crescent or full moon.

Altar in front of East

1. 3 White Candles, forming a Triangle on the table and 1 White Candle that will be used by you for the consecration by fire;
2. 1 Myrrh incense on a stick or a high-flying bird feather;

3. 1 Crystal Cup with Mineral Water;
4. 1 Pot with Earth;
5. The Torah opened in Psalm 23;
6. Christ Crucified on the Cross;
7. The Esoteric Pentagram standing on the table;
8. The object (s) to be enshrined in the center of the triangle;
9. 1 Potted plant, preferably a Sunflower.

"Be careful, not believing in the Devil will not protect you from him. The terror is real, it is real. But you will only beat him when you believe! "

The ritual

START OF EXORCISM AND CONSECRATION RITUAL

Do Appendix I, II, III, IV, V, IX and VIII in the sequence, do not change the sequence.

AIR EXORCISM

Facing the East: Rafael.
Holding the myrrh stick incense in your right hand or the high-flying bird feather, recite the following prayer out loud.

PRAYER OF SYLPHES AND AIR SYLLPHIDS

"Spirit of wisdom, whose breath gives and resumes the form of all things; you, before whom the life of beings is a shadow that changes with a passing vapor; you, who rise above the clouds and walk on the wings of the winds; you, who breathe out, and endless spaces are populated; you, who aspire, and everything that comes from you comes back to you: endless movement in eternal stability, be eternally blessed. We praise you and bless you in the mobile empire of created light, shadows, reflections and images, and we constantly aspire to your unchanging and imperishable clarity. Let the ray of your intelligence and the warmth of your love penetrate to us: then what is mobile will be fixed, the shadow will be a body, the spirit of the air will be a soul, the dream will be a thought. And we will no longer be dragged by the storm, but we will hold the reins of the winged horses in the morning and direct the course of the afternoon winds to fly before you. O spirit of spirits, O eternal soul of souls, O imperishable breath of life, O creative breath, O mouth that aspires and exhales the existence of all beings, in the ebb and flow of your eternal word, which is the divine ocean of movement and the truth. Amen".

My father, my **GOD**, my lord! I ask you with all my heart and with all my soul that you now invoke the god of the elementals of the air: **PARVATI, PARVATI, PARVATI**! We invoke you, we call you in the name of the **CHRIST**, for the power of the **CHRIST** and for the majesty of the **CHRIST**.

Grant us the grace to command and order the sylphs and sylphs in the air.

Make the father, son and holy spirit cross facing the East by blowing the smoke of myrrh incense or high-flying bird feather in each direction of the cross.

Make the cross of the father, the son and the holy spirit facing the South by blowing the smoke of myrrh incense or the feather of a high-flying bird in each direction of the cross.

Make the cross of the father, the son and the holy spirit facing the West, blowing the smoke of myrrh incense or the feather of a high-flying bird in each direction of the cross.

Make the father, son and holy spirit cross facing the North by blowing the smoke from myrrh incense or high-flying bird feather in each direction of the cross.

Facing the East: Rafael.

Spiritus dei ferebatur super aquas et inspirauit in facien hominis spiraculum vitae.

Sit **MICHAEL** dux meus et **SABATABIEL** servus meus in luce et per lucem.

Fiat verbum halitus meus et imperabo spiritibus aeris hujus et refroenabo equos solis voluntate cordis mei et cogitatione mentis meae et nutu oculi dextri.

Exorciso igitur te, creatura aeris, per pentagrammaton et in nomine tetragrammaton, in quibus sunt volutas firma et fides recta. Amen, sela fiat, so be it!

Obey me, sylphs and sylphs of the air, for the **CHRIST**, for the **CHRIST**, for the **CHRIST**. Amen!

MICHAEL! **SABATABIEL**! Mighty Geniuses!

We ask your permission for the air sylphs and sylphs to perform the following work:

Air sylphs and sylphs, we order you in the name of the **FATHER**, the **SON** and the **HOLY SPIRIT** (make the sign of the cross with the stick of incense or the feather of the high-flying bird over the objects (s) that want to consecrate) to magnetize these talisman (s) and sacred objects so that they serve as accumulators of spiritual strength and their bearers are protected in times of danger, as long as they are faithful to **CHRIST** and the teachings of the venerable white store, amen!

EXORCISM OF FIRE

Facing the south: Michael.
Holding the white candle in your right hand, recite the following prayer out loud.

PRAYER OF FIRE SALAMANDERS

"Immortal, eternal, ineffable and uncreated father of all things, that you are carried in the car without ceasing to travel around the worlds that always turn; dominator of the ethereal immensities, where the throne of your power is erected, and above which your formidable eyes

discover everything and your beautiful and holy ears listen to everything, attend to your children, whom you have loved since the birth of the centuries; for your golden, great and eternal majesty shines above the world and the sky and the stars; you are high above them, O sparkling fire; there, you light yourself and preserve yourself by your own splendor, and inexhaustible streams of light come out of your essence, which nourish your infinite spirit. This infinite spirit nourishes all things and makes this inexhaustible treasure of substance always ready for the generation that elaborates and appropriates the forms that you impregnated it from the beginning. This very holy kings around your throne and who make up your court, O universal father, also take their origin from this spirit! The only! O father of happy mortals and immortals. "You have created, in particular, powers that are wonderfully similar to your eternal thought and your lovely essence; you have established them superior to the angels, who announce your will to the world; finally, you created us in the third order in our elementary empire. Here, our continuous exercise is to praise and worship your desires; here, we burn incessantly aspiring to possess you. The father! O mother! O most tender of mothers! O admirable archetype of motherhood and pure love! O son, flower of the children! O form of all forms, soul, spirit, harmony and number of all things! Amen".

My father, my **GOD**, my lord! I ask you with all my heart and with all my soul that you now invoke the god of the fire elementals: **AGNI**, **AGNI**, **AGNI**! We invoke you, we call you in the name of the **CHRIST**, for the power of the **CHRIST** and for the majesty of the **CHRIST**.

Grant us the grace to command and order the fire salamanders.

MICHAEL, KING OF THE SUN and THE RAY;
SAMAEL, KING OF VOLCANOES;
ANAEL, PRINCE of LIGHT ASTRAL;

Assist us in the name of the **CHRIST**, by the power of the **CHRIST**, by the majesty of the **CHRIST**, amen!

Facing the east, where is the altar with the object. With the white candle lit over the object (s) to be consecrated, say:

FIRE Salamanders, we order you in the name of the **FATHER**, the **SON** and the **HOLY SPIRIT** (make the sign of the cross with the white candle on the object (s) you want to consecrate) to magnetize these talisman (s) and sacred objects so that they serve as accumulators of spiritual strength and their bearers are protected in times of danger, as long as they are faithful to **CHRIST** and the teachings of the venerable white store, amen!

WATER EXORCISM

Facing the West: Gabriel.
Holding a crystal bowl with mineral water in your right hand, recite the following prayer out loud.

PRAYER OF THE WAVES AND NEREIDES OF THE WATER

"Terrible king of the sea, you who have the keys to the waterfalls of heaven and who enclose the groundwater in the caves of the earth; king of the flood and the rains of spring, to you who open the springs of rivers and springs, to you who order the moisture, which is like the blood of the earth, to become the sap of plants, we adore you and we invoke. To us, your movable and variable creatures, speak to us in the great turmoil of the sea, and we will tremble before you; speak to us also in the murmur of clear waters, and we will desire your love. O immensity in which all rivers of being, which are always reborn in you, will be lost! O ocean of infinite perfections! Height that you look at in the depth; depth that you exhale at the time, lead us to true life through intelligence and love! Lead us to immortality through sacrifice, so that we may be considered worthy to offer you, one day, water, blood and tears, for the remission of errors. Amen".

My father, my **GOD**, my lord! I ask you with all my heart and with all my soul that you now invoke the god of the water elementals: **VARUNA**, **VARUNA**, **VARUNA**!

We invoke you, we call you in the name of the **CHRIST**, for the power of the **CHRIST** and for the majesty of the **CHRIST**.

Grant us the grace to order and order the waves and nereids of the water.

Fiat firmamentum in medio aquarum et separet aquas ab aquis.

Quae superius sicut quae inferius et quae inferius sicut quae superius, ad perpetranda miracula rei unius.

Sol ejus pater est, luna mater et ventus hunc gestavit in útero suo.

Ascendit terra ad coelum et rursus coelho in terra descendit.

Exorciso te, criatura aquae, ut sis mihi speculum dei vivi in operibus ejus, et fons vitae, et ablutio peccatorum, Amen!

VARUNA! **NICKSA**! Mighty Geniuses!

We ask your permission for the water ripples and nereids to perform the following work:

Facing the east, where is the altar with the object.

Waves and nereids of the water, we order you in the name of the **FATHER**, the **SON** and the **HOLY SPIRIT** (make the sign of the cross with the crystal cup on the object (s) you want to consecrate) to magnetize these talisman (s) and sacred objects so that they serve as accumulators of spiritual strength and their bearers are protected in times of danger, as long as they are faithful to **CHRIST** and the teachings of the venerable white store, amen!

EARTH EXORCISM

Facing the North: Uriel.

Holding a pot of earth in your right hand, recite the following prayer aloud.

PRAYER OF EARTH GNOMES AND PIGMEUSES

"Invisible king, who took the earth for support and dug its depths to fill them with your omnipotence; you, whose name makes the vaults of the world tremble, you who make the seven metals run in the veins of the stones, monarch of the seven lights, remunerator of the underground workers, take us to the desirable air and the kingdom of clarity. We watch and work tirelessly, we search and wait, for the twelve stones of the holy city, for the talismans that are hidden, for the magnet stud that crosses the center of the world. Lord, Lord, Lord, have mercy on those who suffer, unburden our breasts, untangle and lift our heads, magnify us. O stability and movement, O day wrapped in night, O darkness covered with light! O lord, that you never withhold the wages of your workers with you! O Argentine whiteness, O golden splendor! O crown of living and melodious diamonds! You who carry the sky on your finger, with a sapphire ring, you who hide beneath the earth, the kingdom of stones, the wonderful seed of the stars, live, reign and be the eternal dispenser of the riches of which you have made us guardians. Amen".

My father, my **GOD**, my lord! I ask you with all my heart and with all my soul that you now invoke the god of the elementals of the earth: **KITICHI**, **KITICHI**, **KITICHI**! We invoke you, we call you in the name of the **CHRIST**, for the power of the **CHRIST** and for the majesty of the **CHRIST**.

Grant us the grace to rule and order the gnomes and pygmies of the land.

In the name of the 12 stones of the holy city, for the hidden talismans and for the magnet stud that crosses the world, I summon you underground workers of the earth, obey me in the name of **CHRIST**, for the power of **CHRIST** and for the majesty of **CHRIST**.

GOB! **ARBARMANN**! **KITICHI**! Mighty Geniuses!

We ask your permission for the gnomes and pygmies of the land to perform the following work:

Facing the east, where is the altar with the object.

Earth gnomes and pygmies, we ordain you in the name of the **FATHER**, the **SON** and the **HOLY SPIRIT** (make the sign of the cross with the earthen pot on the object (s) you want to consecrate) to magnetize these talisman (s) and sacred objects so that they serve as accumulators of spiritual strength and their bearers are protected in times of danger, as long as they are faithful to **CHRIST** and the teachings of the venerable white store, amen!

Do Appendix VI and I in sequence, do not change the sequence.

End of Exorcism and Consecration Ritual.

Chapter 3

Angelic Evocation Ceremonial Magic

Evocatory Ritual Script
Angel CAHETEL

Ruling Planet: Neptune
Choir: Seraphim
Prince: Mettraton

Born on Days: March 27 - June 8 - August 20 - November 1 - January 13

Virtues granted:

- Blessings from God, expel evil spirits.
- Abundant agricultural crops.

- Inspiration to discover God in ourselves and others.
- Love of work.
- Assistance against spells and enchantments designed to produce sterility in the fields.

Material you will need at the main altar:

- Candles: 1 white on the top and 2 white on the bottom, forming a triangle with the manifestation board in the center;
- The crystal ball in the center of the board;
- Incense: [Cinnamon, laurel, jasmine, benzoin, lemon peel].

Ritual Day and Time

When the moon is growing or full, any day of the week, always from 02:20 to 02:40, start the ceremony 1 hour before, go doing the ritualistic without haste, when it is that time, open the veil.

Place the seal on the main altar.

Starting the ritual

- Light the candles and incense on the altar of the manifestations;

- Read and do Appendices I, II, III, IV, V, IX and VIII in sequence, do not change the sequence;

Discourse to Angels

- Facing the EAST;
- Preparations for the First Conjuration:

  Take a deep breath and vocalize the Angel's mantra as written, out loud until there is no more air in your lungs, repeat 3x:

KERRAAAAAAATTTTTTTT

Repeat 3x the Angel's Psalm in Latin

> *"Venite adoremus et procidamusante Deum, ploremus coram Domino qui fecit nos."*

Recite aloud the Psalm (s) of the Angel in the Torah:

Psalm 94

1O God of vengeance, O Lord; O God show vengeance.

2Exalt Yourself, O Judge of the earth, render to the haughty their recompense.

3How long will the wicked, O Lord, how long will the wicked rejoice?

4They spout forth, they speak falsely; all workers of violence boast.

5Your people, O Lord, they crush, and Your inheritance they afflict.

6They slay the widow and the stranger, and they murder the orphans.

7They say, "Yah will not see, nor will the God of Jacob understand."

8Understand, [you] most boorish of the people, and [you] fools, when will you gain intelligence?

9Will He Who implants the ear not hear or will He Who forms the eye not see?

10Will He Who chastises nations not reprove? [He is] the One Who teaches man knowledge.

11The Lord knows man's thoughts that they are vanity.

12Fortunate is the man whom You, Yah, chastise, and from Your Torah You teach him.

13To grant him peace from days of evil, while a pit is dug for the wicked.

14For the Lord will not forsake His people, nor will He desert His inheritance.

15For until righteousness will judgment return,

and after it all those upright in heart.

16Who will rise up for me against evildoers; who will stand up for me against workers of violence?

17Had not the Lord been my help, in an instant my soul would rest silent.

18If I said, "My foot has slipped," Your kindness, O Lord, supported me.

19With my many thoughts within me, Your consolations cheered me.

20Will the throne of evil join You, which iniquity for a statute?

21They gather upon the soul of the righteous and condemn innocent blood.

22But the Lord was my fortress, and my God the rock of my refuge.

23And He returned upon them their violence, and for their evil, may He cut them off; may the Lord our God cut them off.

Psalm 95

1Come, let us sing praises to the Lord; let us shout to the rock of our salvation.

2Let us greet His presence with thanksgiving; let us shout to Him with songs.

3For the Lord is a great God and a great King over all divine powers.

4In Whose hand are the depths of the earth, and the heights of the mountains are His.

5For the sea is His, He made it, and His hands formed the dry land.

6Come, let us prostrate ourselves and bow; let us kneel before the Lord, our Maker.

7For He is our God, and we are the people of His pasture and the flocks of His hand, today, if you hearken to His voice.

8Do not harden your heart as [in] Meribah, as [on] the day of Massah in the desert.

9When your ancestors tested Me; they tried Me, even though they had seen My work.

10Forty years I quarreled with a generation, and I said, "They are a people of erring hearts and they did not know My ways."

11For which reason I swore in My wrath, that they would not enter My resting place.

Opening the Veil

Read and do Appendix X and XI

Prayer

"**CAHETEL**, I received from you, Lord, infinite gifts. My lips easily express the world that You have created and my hands shape your primordial matter in graceful forms. You have allowed me to triumph, Oh **CAHETEL**! You have located around me a court of flatterers that you have placed between You and me, ditches, gardens, lands, properties, obstacles that keep me away from Your divine presence. However, you have also put me in Mr. **CAHETEL** the ardor to overcome them. Allow me, Lord, that this ardor be the strongest, the most intense in me so that I can give thanks for this and, thus, come to jump ditches, circumvent enclosures, pull me out of the beauties of the gardens of the earth, overcome adulation, triumphs, fame and run to your source of life. Deliver me, Lord, from vanity, and I will be freed from the bondage of abundance ".

Read and do Appendix VI, VII and I in sequence, do not change the sequence.

End of Ritual

[cahetEL - Angelic Magic with the Kabbalistic Angel cahetEL], from [Frater Eisenheim]

Conclusion

I hope this book has helped you to speak with the holy angels of the God of Abraham. I also hope that you will succeed in the rituals and that you will increasingly want to enter the 7 heavens of the prophet Enoch, learning more and more about these beings of Light and all the angelic kingdoms.

With the help of holy angels and heavenly spirits, you will be able to grow and develop your full potential. You will discover the purpose of living, even taking the beatings that life usually gives in the trajectory, living is not easy, but everything in life there is a reason, there is no chance, everything that happens in our life happens for a reason, which you will surely discover . I wish you had more contact with the divine nature, when I started my journey, believe me, I did not know how to pray our Father, but my Faith, persistence and dedication have brought me here.

All aspects of your life will evolve when you open your mind and heart to the angelic realms, one of the reasons that made me write this book is that I have noticed people's growing interest in making pacts with demons, believe me, you don't have to make a pact with the devil to solve your problem, if what you want is within the law, it will be granted. Practice White Magic and see the supernatural happen in your life, I wish you great joy and happiness in the search.

Shalom.
Eisenheim.

APPENDIX I

LESSER BANISHING RITUAL OF THE PENTAGRAM

Facing the East: Rafael.

Kabbalistic Cross

Touch the forehead with your index finger saying **ATAH**

Touch the navel with your index finger saying **MALKUTH**

Touch the right shoulder with your index finger saying **VE GEBURAH**

Touch the left shoulder with the index finger saying **VE GEDULAH**

Put both hands together and raise them high above your head saying **LE-OLAM**

Lower both hands and place them over your heart saying **AMEN**!

Formation of the Pentagram

Make the pentagram below with your index finger following the direction of the arrow:

BANISHING

When done, point to the center of the pentagram and vibrate the name of the divine: **YOD HE VAU HE**

Turn to the South. Michael.

Make the pentagram below with your index finger following the direction of the arrow:

BANISHING

When done, point to the center of the pentagram and vibrate the name of the divine: **ADONAI**

Turn to the West: Gabriel.

Make the pentagram below with your index finger following the direction of the arrow:

Begin here

BANISHING

When done, point to the center of the pentagram and vibrate the name of the divine: **EHEIEH**

Turn to the North: Uriel.

Make the pentagram below with your index finger following the direction of the arrow:

Begin here

BANISHING

When done, point to the center of the pentagram and vibrate the name of the divine: **AGLA**

The Evocation of the Archangels

> *Facing the East: Rafael.*

> Open your arms in the shape of a cross and

say:

> In front of me **RA-PHA-EL**

> Behind me **GA-BRI-EL**

> To my right **MI-CHA-EL**

> On my left **U-RI-EL**

The pentagrams flash around me and the six-rayed star above me.

Kabbalistic Cross

Touch the forehead with your index finger saying **ATAH**

Touch the navel with your index finger saying **MALKUTH**

Touch the right shoulder with your index finger saying **VE GEBURAH**

Touch the left shoulder with the index finger saying **VE GEDULAH**

Put both hands together and raise them high above your head saying **LE-OLAM**

Lower both hands and place them over your heart saying **AMEN**!

APPENDIX II

LESSER INVOKING RITUAL OF THE PENTAGRAM

Facing the East: Rafael.

Kabbalistic Cross

Touch the forehead with your index finger saying **ATAH**

Touch the navel with your index finger saying **MALKUTH**

Touch the right shoulder with your index finger saying **VE GEBURAH**

Touch the left shoulder with the index finger saying **VE GEDULAH**

Put both hands together and raise them high above your head saying **LE-OLAM**

Lower both hands and place them over your heart saying **AMEN**!

Formation of the Pentagram

Facing the East: Rafael.

Make the pentagram below with your index finger following the direction of the arrow:

When done, point to the center of the pentagram and vibrate the name of the divine: **YOD HE VAU HE**

Turn to the South. Michael.

Make the pentagram below with your index finger following the direction of the arrow:

Begin here

INVOKING

When done, point to the center of the pentagram and vibrate the name of the divine**: ADONAI**

Turn to the West: Gabriel.

Make the pentagram below with your index finger following the direction of the arrow:

INVOKING

When done, point to the center of the pentagram and vibrate the name of the divine: **EHEIEH**

Turn to the North: Uriel.

Make the pentagram below with your index finger following the direction of the arrow:

Begin here

INVOKING

When done, point to the center of the pentagram and vibrate the name of the divine: **AGLA**

The Evocation of the Archangels

Facing the East: Rafael.

Open your arms in the shape of a cross and say:

In front of me **RA-PHA-EL**

Behind me **GA-BRI-EL**

To my right **MI-CHA-EL**

On my left **U-RI-EL**

The pentagrams flash around me and the six-rayed star above me.

Kabbalistic Cross

Touch the forehead with your index finger saying **ATAH**

Touch the navel with your index finger saying **MALKUTH**

Touch the right shoulder with your index finger saying **VE GEBURAH**

Touch the left shoulder with the index finger saying **VE GEDULAH**

Put both hands together and raise them high above your head saying **LE-OLAM**

Lower both hands and place them over your heart saying **AMEN**!

APPENDIX III

CONJURATION OF THE FOUR

Facing the East: Rafael.

Caput mortum, imperet tibi dominus per vivum et devotum serpentem!

Cherub, imperet tibi dominus per Adam **JOT-CHAVAH**.

Aquila errans, imperet tibi dominus per alas tauri!

Serpens, imperet tibi dominus **TETRAGRAMATON**, per angelum et leonem!

MICHAEL, GABRIEL, RAPHAEL, URIEL, FLUAT UDOR per spiritum **ELOHIM**.

MANEAT in **TERRA** per adam **JOT-CHAVAH**.

FIAT FIRMAMENTUM per **IEHOVAH-SABAOTH**.

FIAT JUDICIUM per ignem in virtute **MICHAEL**.

Angel of the blind eyes, obey, or pass away with this holy water!

Work winged bull, or revert to the earth, unless thou wilt that I should pierce thee with this sword!

Chained eagle, obey my sign, or fly before this breath!

Writhing serpent, crawl at my feet, or be tortured by the sacred fire and give way before the perfumes that I burn in it!

Water, return to water!

Fire, burn!

Air, circulate!

Earth, revert to earth!

By virtue of the pentagram, which is the morning star, and by the name of the tetragram, which is written in the center of the cross of light!

Amen. Amen. Amen.

APPENDIX IV

CONJURATION OF THE SEVEN

Facing the East: Rafael.

In the name of **MICHAEL**, may **IEHOVAH** command thee and drive thee hence, **CHAVA-JOTH**!

In the name of **GABRIEL**, may **ADONAI** command thee, and drive thee hence, **BAEL**!

In the name of **RAPHAEL**, begone before **ELIAL**, **SANGABIEL**!

By **SAMAEL SABAOTH**, and in the name of **ELOHIM GHIBOR**, get thee hence, **ANDRAMELEKH**!

By **ZAKHARIEL** and **SAKHIEL MELEKH**, be obedient unto **ELVAH, SANAGABRIL**!

By the divine and human name of **SHADDAI**, and by the sign of the pentagram that I hold in my right hand, in the name of the angel **ANAEL**, by the power of Adam and Eve, who are **JOT-CHAVAH**, begone **LILITH**!

Let us rest in peace, **NAHEMAH**!

By the holy **ELOHIM** and by the names of the Genii **KASHIEL, SEHALTIEL, APHIEL** and **TZARAHIEL**, at the command of **ORIPHIEL**, depart from us **MOLOKH**! We deny thee our children to devour! Amen. Amen. Amen.

APPENDIX V

THE QABALISTICAL INVOCATION OF THE KING SOLOMON

Facing the East: Rafael.

POWERS of the Kingdom, be beneath my left foot, and within my right hand.

Glory and Eternity touch my shoulders, and guide me in the Paths of Victory.

Mercy and justice be ye the Equilibrium and splendour of my life.

Understanding and Wisdom give unto me the Crown.

Spirits of Malkuth conduct me between the two columns whereon is supported the whole edifice of the Temple.

Angels of Netzach and of Hod strengthen me upon the Cubical Stone of Yesod.

O **GEDULAHEL**! O **GEBURAHEL**! O **TIPHERETH**!

BINAHEL, be Thou my Love!

RUACH CHOKMAHEL, be Thou my Light!

Be that which Thou art, and that which thou willest to be, O **KETHERIEL**!

Ishim, assist me in the Name Of **SHADDAL**

Cherubim, be my strength in the Name of **ADONAI**

Beni Elohim, be ye my brethren in the Name of the Son, and by the virtues of **TZABAOTH**.

Elohim, fight for me in the Name of **TETRAGRAMMATON**.

Malachim, protect me in the Name Of **YOD HE VAU HE**.

Seraphim, purify my love in the Name of **ELOAH**.

Chaschmalim, enlighten me with the splendours of **ELOHI**, and of **SCHECHINAH**.

Aralim, act ye; Auphanim, revolve and shine.

Chaioth Ha-Qadosch, cry aloud, speak, roar, and groan; Qadosch, Qadosch, Qadosch., **SHADDAI**, **ADONAI**, **YOD CHAVAH**, **EHEIEH ASHER EHEIEH**!

Halelu-Yah! Halelu-Yah! Halelu-Yah. Amen!Amen! Amen!

APPENDIX VI

THE LICENSE TO DEPART

Facing the East: Rafael.

Because ye have been obedient, and have obeyed the commandments of the Creator, feel and inhale this grateful odour, and afterwards depart ye unto your abodes and retreats; be there peace between us and you; be ye ever ready to come when ye shall be cited and called; and may the blessing of God, as far as ye are capable of receiving it, be upon you, provided ye be obedient and prompt to come unto us without solemn rites and observances on our part. In the Name of **ADONAI**, the Eternal and Everlasting One, let each of you return unto his place; be there peace between us and you, and be ye ready to come when ye are called. Amem.

APPENDIX VII

Cleaning the Environment

Removing Evil Spirits from the Environment

Facing the East: Rafael.

Psalm 23

1A song of David. The Lord is my shepherd; I shall not want.
2He causes me to lie down in green pastures; He leads me beside still waters.
3He restores my soul; He leads me in paths of righteousness for His name's sake.
4Even when I walk in the valley of darkness, I will fear no evil for You are with me; Your rod and Your staff-they comfort me.
5You set a table before me in the presence of my adversaries; You anointed my head with oil; my cup overflows.
6May only goodness and kindness pursue me all the days of my life, and I will dwell in the house of the Lord for length of days.

Psalm 91

1He who dwells in the covert of the Most High will lodge in the shadow of the Almighty.

2I shall say of the Lord [that He is] my shelter and my fortress, my God in Whom I trust.

3For He will save you from the snare that traps from the devastating pestilence.

4With His wing He will cover you, and under His wings you will take refuge; His truth is an encompassing shield.

5You will not fear the fright of night, the arrow that flies by day;

6Pestilence that prowls in darkness, destruction that ravages at noon.

7A thousand will be stationed at your side, and ten thousand at your right hand; but it will not approach you.

8You will but gaze with your eyes, and you will see the annihilation of the wicked.

9For you [said], "The Lord is my refuge"; the Most High you made your dwelling.

10No harm will befall you, nor will a plague draw near to your tent.

11For He will command His angels on your behalf to guard you in all your ways.

12On [their] hands they will bear you, lest your foot stumble on a stone.

13On a young lion and a cobra you will tread; you will trample the young lion and the serpent.

14For he yearns for Me, and I shall rescue him; I

shall fortify him because he knows My name.

<u>15</u>He will call Me and I shall answer him; I am with him in distress; I shall rescue him and I shall honor him.

<u>16</u>With length of days I shall satiate him, and I shall show him My salvation.

APPENDIX VIII

Prayer

Facing the East: Rafael.

ADONAI, **ELOHIM**, **EL**, **EHEIEH ASHER EHEIEH**, Prince of Princes, Existence of Existences, have mercy upon me **ABBA**, and cast Thine eyes upon Thy Servant, who invokes Thee most devoutedly, and supplicates Thee by Thy Holy and tremendous Name **TETRAGRAMMATON** to be propitious, and to order Thine Angels and Spirits to come and take up their abode in this place; O ye Angels and Spirits of the Stars, O all ye Angels and Elementary Spirits, O all ye Spirits present before the Face of God, I the Minister and faithful Servant of the Most High conjure ye, let God Himself, the Existence of Existences, conjure ye to come and be present at this Operation, I, the Servant of God, most humbly entreat ye. Amen.

APPENDIX IX

CONFESSION

Facing the East: Rafael.

O LORD of Heaven and of Earth, before Thee do I confess my sins, and lament them, cast down and humbled in Thy presence. For I have sinned before Thee by pride, avarice, and boundless desire of honours and riches; by idleness, gluttony, greed, debauchery, and drunkenness; because I have offended Thee by all kinds of sins of the flesh, adulteries, and pollutions, which I have committed myself, and consented that others should commit; by sacrilege, thefts, rapine, violation, and homicide; by the evil use I have made of my possessions, by my prodigality, by the sins which I have committed against Hope and Charity, by my evil advice, flatteries, bribes, and the ill distribution which I have made of the goods of which I have been possessed; by repulsing and maltreating the poor, in the distribution which I have made of the goods committed to my charge, by afflicting those over whom I have been set in authority, by not visiting the prisoners, by depriving the dead of burial, by not receiving the poor, by neither feeding the hungry nor giving drink to the thirsty, by never keeping the Sabbath and the other feasts, by not living chastely and piously on those days, by the easy consent which I have given to those who incited me to evil deeds, by injuring instead of aiding those who demanded help from me, by refusing to give ear unto the cry of the poor, by not respecting the aged, by not keeping my word, by disobedience to my parents, by ingratitude towards those from whom I have received kindness, by indulgence in sensual pleasures, by irreverent behaviour in the Temple of God, by unseemly gestures thereat, by entering therein without reverence, by vain and unprofitable discourse when there, by despising the sacred vessels of the temple, by turning the holy Ceremonies into ridicule, by touching and eating the sacred bread with impure lips and with profane hands, and by the neglect of my prayers and adorations. I detest also the crimes which I have committed by evil thoughts, vain and impure meditations, false suspicions, and rash judgments; by the evil consent which I have readily given unto the advice of the wicked, by lust of impure and sensual pleasures; by my idle words, my lies, and my deceit; by my false vows in various ways; and by my continual slander and calumny. I detest also the crimes which I have committed within; the treachery and discord which I have incited; my curiosity, greed, false speaking, violence, malediction, murmurs, blasphemies, vain words, insults, dissimulations; my sins against God by the transgression of the ten commandments, by neglect of my duties and obligations, and by want of love towards God and towards my neighbour. Furthermore, I hate the sins which I have committed in all my senses, by sight, by hearing, by taste, by smell, and by touch, in every way that human weakness can offend the Creator; by my carnal thoughts, deeds, and meditations. In which I humbly confess that I have sinned, and recognise myself as being in the sight of God the most criminal of all men. I accuse myself before Thee, O God, and I adore Thee with all humility. O ye, Holy Angels, and ye, Children of God, in your presence I publish my sins, so that mine Enemy may have no advantage over me, and may not be able to reproach me at the last day; that he may not be able to say that I have concealed my sins, and that 1 be not then accused in the presence of the Lord; but, on the contrary, that on my account there may be joy in Heaven, as over the just who have confessed their sins in thy presence. O Most Mighty and All Powerful Father, grant through Thine unbounded Mercy that I may both see and know all the Spirits which I invoke, so that by their means I may see my will and desire accomplished, by Thy Sovereign grandeur, and by Thine Ineffable and

Eternal Glory, Thou Who art and Who wilt be for ever the Pure and Ineffable Father of All.

Prayer

O Lord All Powerful, Eternal God and Father of all Creatures, shed upon me the Divine Influence of Thy Mercy, for I am Thy Creature. I beseech Thee to defend me from mine Enemies, and to confirm in me true and steadfast faith. O Lord, I commit my Body and my Soul unto Thee, seeing I put my trust in none beside Thee; it is on Thee alone that I rely; O Lord my God aid me; O Lord hear me in the day and hour wherein I shall invoke Thee. I pray Thee by Thy Mercy not to put me in oblivion, nor to remove me from Thee. O Lord be Thou my succour, Thou Who art the God of my salvation. O Lord make me a new heart according unto Thy loving Kindness. These, O Lord, are the gifts which I await from Thee, O my God and my Master, Thou Who livest and reignest unto the Ages of the Ages. Amen. O Lord God the All Powerful One, Who hast formed unto Thyself great and Ineffable Wisdom, and Co-eternal with Thyself before the countless Ages; Thou Who in the Birth of Time hast created the Heavens, and the Earth, the Sea, and things that they contain; Thou Who hast vivified all things by the Breath of Thy Mouth, I praise Thee, I bless Thee, I adore Thee, and I glorify Thee. Be Thou propitious unto me who am but a miserable sinner, and despise me not; save me and succour me) even me the work of Thine hands. I conjure and entreat Thee by Thy Holy Name to banish from my Spirit the darkness of Ignorance, and to enlighten me with the Fire of Thy Wisdom; take away from me all evil desires, and let not my speech be as that of the foolish. O Thou, God the Living One, Whose Glory, Honour, and Kingdom shall extend unto the Ages of the Ages. Amen.

APPENDIX X

Here be the Symbols of Secret things, the standards, the ensigns, and the banners, of God the Conqueror; and the arms of the Almighty One, to compel the Aerial Potencies. I command ye absolutely by their power and virtue that ye come near unto us, into our presence, from whatsoever part of the world ye may be in, and that ye delay not to obey us in all things wherein we shall command ye by the virtue of God the Mighty One. Come ye promptly, and delay not to appear, and answer us with humility. Here again I conjure ye and most urgently command ye; I force, constrain, and exhort ye to the utmost, by the most mighty and powerful Name of God **EL**, strong and wonderful, and by God the just and Upright, I exorcise ye and command ye that ye in no way delay, but that ye come immediately and upon the instant hither before us, without noise, deformity, or hideousness, but with all manner of gentleness and mildness. I exorcise ye anew, and powerfully conjure ye, commanding ye with strength and violence by Him Who spake and it was done; and by all these names: **EL SHADDAI**, **ELOHIM**, **ELOHI**, **TZABAOTH**, **ELIM**, **ASHER EHEIEH**, **YAH**, **TETRAGRAMMATON**, **SHADDAI**, which signify God the High and Almighty, the God of Israel, through Whom undertaking all our operations we shall prosper in all the works of our hands, seeing that the Lord is now, always, and for ever with us, in our heart and in our lips; and by His Holy Names, and by the virtue of the Sovereign God, we shall accomplish all our work. Come ye at once without any hideousness or deformity before us, come ye without monstrous appearance, in a gracious form or figure. Come ye, for we exorcise ye with the utmost vehemence by the Name of **IAH** and **ON**, which Adam spake and heard; by the Name **EL**, which Noah heard, and saved himself with all his family from the Deluge; by the Name **IOD**, which Noah heard, and knew God the Almighty One; by the Name **AGLA** which Jacob heard, and saw the Ladder which touched Heaven, and the Angels who ascended and descended upon it, whence he called that place the House of God and the Gate of Heaven; and by the Name **ELOHIM**, and in the Name **ELOHIM**, which Moses named, invoked, and heard in Horeb the Mount of God, and he was found worthy to hear Him speak from the Burning Bush; and by the Name **AIN SOPH**, which Aaron heard, and was at once made eloquent, wise, and learned; and by the Name **TZABAOTH**, which Moses named and invoked, and all the ponds and rivers were covered with blood throughout the land of Egypt; and by the Name **IOD**, which Moses named and invoked, and striking upon the dust of the earth both men and beasts were struck with disease; and by the Name, and in the Name **PRIMEUMATON** which Moses named and invoked, and there fell a great and severe hail throughout all the land of Egypt, destroying the vines, the trees, and the woods which were in that country; and by the Name **IAPHAR**, which Moses heard and invoked, and immediately a great pestilence began to appear through all the land of Egypt, striking and slaying the asses, the oxen, and the sheep of the Egyptians, so that they all died; and by the Name **ABADDON** which Moses invoked and sprinkled the dust towards heaven, and immediately there fell so great rain upon the men, cattle, and flocks, that they all died throughout the land of Egypt; and by the Name **ELION** which Moses invoked, and there fell so great hail as had never been seen from the beginning of the world unto that time, so that all men, and herds, and everything that was in the fields perished and died throughout all the land of Egypt. And by the Name **ADONAI**, which Moses having invoked, there came so great a quantity of locusts which appeared in the land of Egypt, that they devoured and swallowed up all that the hail had spared; and by the Name of **PATHEON**, which having invoked, there arose so thick, so awful, and so terrible darkness throughout the land of Egypt, during the space of three days and three nights, that almost all who were left alive died; and by the Name

YESOD, and in the Name **YESOD**, which Moses invoked, and at midnight all the first-born, both of men and of animals, died; and by the Name Of **YESHIMON**, which Moses named and invoked, and the Red Sea divided itself and separated in two; and by the Name **HESION**, which Moses invoked, and all the army of Pharaoh was drowned in the waters; and by the Name **ANABONA**, which Moses having heard upon Mount Sinai, he was found worthy to receive and obtain the tables of stone written with the finger of God the Creator; and by the Name **ERYGION**, which Joshua having invoked when he fought against the Moabites, he defeated them and gained the victory; and by the Name **HOA**, and in the Name **HOA**, which David invoked, and he was delivered from the hand of Goliath; and by the Name **YOD**, which Solomon having named and invoked, he was found worthy to ask for and to obtain in sleep the Ineffable Wisdom of God; and by the Name **YIAI**, which Solomon having named and invoked, he was found worthy to have power over all the Demons, Potencies, Powers, and Virtues of the Air. I conjure ye anew by that most Holy Name which the whole Universe fears, respects, and reveres, which is written by these letters and characters, **IOD**, **HE**, **VAU**, **HE**; and by the last and terrible judgment; by the Seat of **BALDACHIA**; and by this Holy Name, **YIAI**, which Moses invoked, and there followed that great judgment of God, when Dathan and Abiram were swallowed up in the centre of the earth. Otherwise, if ye contravene and resist us by your disobedience unto the virtue and power of this Name **YIAI**, we curse ye even unto the Depth of the Great Abyss, into the which we shall cast, hurl, and bind ye, if ye show yourselves rebellious against the Secret of Secrets, and against the Mystery of Mysteries. AMEN, AMEN. FIAT, FIAT. I conjure ye anew, I constrain and command ye with the utmost vehemence and power, by that most potent and powerful Name of God, **EL**, strong and wonderful, by Him Who spake and it was done; and by the Name **IAH**, which Moses heard, and spoke with God; and by the Name **AGLA**, which Joseph invoked, and was delivered out of the hands of his brethren; and by the Name **VAU**, which Abraham heard, and knew God the Almighty One; and by the Name of Four Letters, **TETRAGRAMMATON**, which Joshua named and invoked, and he was rendered worthy and found deserving to lead the Army of Israel into the Promised Land; and by the Name **ANABONA**, by which God formed Man and the whole Universe; and by the Name **ARPHETON**, and in the Name **ARPHETON**, by which the Angels who are destined to that end will summon the Universe, in visible body and form, and will assemble (all people) together by the sound of the Trumpet at that terrible and awful Day of judgment, when the memory of the wicked and ungodly shall perish; and by the Name **ADONAI**, by which God will judge all human flesh, at Whose voice all men, both good and evil, will rise again, and all men and Angels will assemble in the air before the Lord, Who will judge and condemn the wicked; and by the Name **ONEIPHETON**, by which God will summon the dead, and raise them up again unto life; and by the Name **ELOHIM**, and in the Name **ELOHIM**, by which God will disturb and excite tempests throughout all the seas, so that they will cast out the fish therefrom, and in one day the third part of men about the sea and the rivers shall die; and by the Name **ELOHI**, and in the Name **ELOHI**, by which God will dry up the sea and the rivers, so that men can go on foot through their channels; and by the Name **ON**, and in the Name **ON**, by which God will restore and replace the sea, the rivers, the streams, and the brooks, in their previous state; and by the Name **MESSIACH**, and in the Name **MESSIACH**, by which God will make all animals combat together, so that they shall die in a single day; and by the Name **ARIEL**, by which God will destroy in a single day all buildings, so that there shall not be left one stone upon another; and by the Name **IAHT**, by which God will cast one stone upon another, so that all people and nations will fly from the sea-shore, and will say unto them cover us and hide us; and by the Name **EMANUEL**, by which God will perform wonders, and the winged creatures and birds of the air shall contend with one another; and by the Name **ANAEL**, and in the Name **ANAEL**, by which God will cast down the mountains and fill up the valleys, so that the surface of the earth shall be level in all parts; and by the Name **ZEDEREZA**, and in the Name **ZEDEREZA**, by which God will cause the Sun and Moon to be darkened, and the Stars of heaven to fall; and by the Name **SEPHERIEL**, by which God will come to Universal judgment, like a Prince newly crowned entering in triumph into his capital city, girded with a zone of gold, and preceded by Angels, and at His aspect all climes and parts of the Universe shall be troubled and astonished, and a fire shall go forth before Him, and flames and storms shall surround Him; and by the Name **TAU**, by which God brought the Deluge, and the waters prevailed above the mountains, and fifteen cubits above their summits; and by the Name **RUACHIAH**, by which God having purged the Ages, He will make His Holy Spirit to descend upon the Universe, and will cast ye, ye rebellious Spirits, and unclean beings, into the Depths of the Lake of the Abyss, in misery, filth, and mire, and will place ye in impure and foul dungeons bound with eternal chains of fire. By these Names then, and by all the other Holy Names of God before Whom no man can stand and live, and which Names the armies of the Demons fear, tremble at, and shudder; we conjure ye, we potently exorcise and command ye, conjuring ye in addition by the terrible and tremendous **PATHS** of **GOD** and by His Holy habitation wherein He reigneth and commandeth unto the eternal Ages. Amen. By the virtue of all these aforesaid, we command ye that ye remain not in any place wherein ye are, but to come hither promptly without delay to do that which we shall enjoin ye. But if ye be still contumacious, we, by the Authority of a Sovereign and Potent God, deprive ye of all quality, condition, degree, and place which ye now enjoy, and precipitate ye into and relegate ye unto the Kingdom of Fire and of Sulphur, to be there eternally tormented. Come ye then from all parts of the earth, wheresoever ye may be, and behold the Symbols and Names of that Triumphant Sovereign Whom all creatures obey, otherwise we shall bind ye and conduct ye in spite of yourselves, into our presence bound with chains of fire, because those effects which proceed and issue from our Science and operation, are ardent with a fire which shall consume and burn ye eternally, for by these the whole Universe trembleth, the earth is moved, the stones thereof rush together, all creatures obey, and the rebellious Spirits are tormented by the power of the Sovereign Creator.

APPENDIX XI

Oh you, powerful, blessed and glorious angel of God (PUT HERE THE NAME OF THE ANGEL), who governs and is a superior angel governing your philosopher's abode, I am the servant of the one who gave you life, your God **EL**, the same that you obey and are the referee's distributor of all things, both in heaven, on earth and in hell, I invoke you, conjure you and I beg you (PUT HERE THE NAME OF THE ANGEL), that appears without delay in virtue and power of the same God **IAH**, I conjure you by the one you obey and is placed as king in the divine power of God, that you immediately descend from your order, or place of residence and come to me and appear visibly in this crystal ball, in yours own form and glory speaking with an intangible voice for my understanding.

Oh you strong and powerful angel (PUT HERE THE NAME OF THE ANGEL), who is commanded by the power of God to rule animals, vegetables and minerals and cause him and all God's creatures to spread and multiply according to the type of nature. I serve the greatest God, whom you obey, I humbly ask and beg you to come from his heavenly mansion and show me all the things I desire from you, as long as you are able or possible to do it and if my **ABBA** allow the same. Oh you, servant of mercy (PUT HERE THE NAME OF THE ANGEL), I humbly plead and beg you for these holy and blessed names of God, I also conjure you in this and this powerful name **ANABONA**, that you appear visibly without delay and clearly in its own form and glory and that it is through that crystal ball, that I can see visibly, can hear you, speak to you before me and can be blessed by your angelic glory and assistance, family friendship and constant companionship of communion and instruction, now and for all time, precisely to inform me and instruct me in ignorance and corrupt truths, by the almighty **ADONAI**, king of the king, the one who grants all gifts, who generously and paternally graces with mercy, pleasing bless me for this reason, oh blessed angel (PUT HERE THE NAME OF THE ANGEL), be friendly before me, as God will give you the power and presence to appear and that I can count on your SAINTS ANGELS, AMEN, AMEN, AMEN!

COME ON SPIRIT, **ADONAI** IS CALLING YOU!COME ON SPIRIT, **YOD HE VAU HE** IS CALLING YOU! COME ON SPIRIT, **EL** IS CALLING YOU!COME ON SPIRIT, **AGLA** AND **ON** IS CALLING YOU!COME ON SPIRIT, **YOSHUA OF NAZARE** IS CALLING YOU!!!!

[cahetEL - Angelic Magic with the Kabbalistic Angel cahetEL], from [Frater Eisenheim]

BIBLIOGRAPHY

APOCRYPHA: Os livros chamados *Apocrypha,* de acordo com a Versão Autorizada. Londres, UK: Oxford University Press, n.d.

BRANDON, S. G. F. *Religion in Ancient History.* London, UK: George Allen and Unwin Limited, 1973.

KABALEB: *Os Deuses Internos – O Programa Profundo dos 72 Gênios da Cabala.* Lisboa, PT: Editora Pergaminho, 2000.

KONSTANTINOS: *Summoning Spirits: The Art of Magical Evocation (Llewellyn's Practical Magick).* Minnesota, EUA: Llewellyn Publications, 2002.

BARRET, Francis: *The Magus,* Book II. London, UK, 1801

LEITCH, Aaron: *The Essential Enochian Grimoire: An Introduction to Angel Magick from Dr. John Dee to the Golden Dawn.* Minnesota, EUA: Llewellyn Publications, 2014.

[cahetEL - Angelic Magic with the Kabbalistic Angel cahetEL], from [Frater Eisenheim]

BROCKINGTON, L. H: *A Critical Introduction to the Apocrypha.* London, UK: Gerald Duckworth and Company Limited, 1961.

BUNSON, Matthew: *Angels A to Z.* New York, NY: Crown Trade Paperbacks, 1996.

BURNHAM, Sophy: *A Book of Angels: Reflections on Angels Past and Present and True Stories of How They Touch Our Lives.* New York, NY: Ballantine Books, 1990.

CONNELL, Jahice T. *Angel Power.* New York, NY: Ballantine Books, 1990.

DAVIDSON, Gustav. *A Dictionary of Angels.* New York, NY: The Free Press, 1967.

FOX, Matthew and Sheldrake, Rupert. *The Physics of Angels: Exploring the Realm Where Science and Spirit Meet.* San Francisco, CA: Harper San Francisco, 1996.

GINZBERG, Louis. *The Legends of the Jews.* Philadelphia, PA: The Jewish Publication Society of America, 1909-1937.

[cahetEL - Angelic Magic with the Kabbalistic Angel cahetEL], from [Frater Eisenheim]

GIOVETTI, Paola. *Angels: The Role of Celestial Guardians and Beings of Light.* York Beach, ME: Samuel Weiser, Inc., 1993.

LÉVI, Éliphas. *Dogma e Ritual da Alta Magia.* São Paulo, SP: Pensamento, 2017.

CROWLEY, Aleister; MATHERS, S L MacGregor. *The Greater and Lesser Keys of Solomon the King.* London, UK: Mockingbird Press, 2016.

HODSON, Geoffrey. *The Angelic Host.* London, UK: The Theosophical Publishing House Limited, 1928.

JONES, Timothy. *Celebration of Angels.* Nashville, TN: Thomas Nelson Publishers, 1994.

MOOLENBURGH, H. C. *A Handbook of Angels.* Saffron Walden, UK: The C. W. Daniel Company Limited, 1984.

RAVENWOLF, Silver. *Angels: Companions in Magic.* St. Paul, MN: Llewellyn Publications, 1996.

WEBSTER, Richard. *Spirit Guides and Angel Guardians.* St. Paul, MN: Llewellyn Publications, 1998.

VACCHIANO, Inácio. *A Cabala de Hakash Ba Hakash*. Disponível em: <https://inaciovacchiano.files.wordpress.com/2018/02/a-cabala-de-hakash-ba-hakash.pdf>. Acesso em: 29 Outubro 2018.

BANZHAF, Hajo; THELER, Brigitte. *Tarô de Crowley - Palavras-chave*. São Paulo, BR: Madras Editora, 2006.

Made in the USA
Monee, IL
02 March 2022

92127822R00062